CULTURE IN ACTION
Architecture

Jane Bingham

www.raintreepublishers.co.uk
Visit our website to find out more information about Raintree books.

To order:

☎ Phone +44 (0) 1865 888066

▤ Fax +44 (0) 1865 314091

▢ Visit www.raintreepublishers.co.uk

Raintree is an imprint of Capstone Global Library Limited, a company incorporated in England and Wales having its registered office at 7 Pilgrim Street, London, EC4V 6LB – Registered company number: 6695582

"Raintree" is a registered trademark of Pearson Education Limited, under licence to Capstone Global Library Limited

Text © Capstone Global Library Limited 2010
First published in hardback in 2010

Edited by Louise Galpine, Rachel Howells, and Helen Cox
Designed by Kimberly Miracle and Betsy Wernert
Original illustrations © Capstone Global Library Ltd.
Illustrated by kja-artists.com
Picture research by Hannah Taylor and Kay Altwegg
Production by Alison Parsons
Originated by Dot Gradations Ltd.
Printed in China by CTPS.

ISBN 978 1 406212 09 9 (hardback)
14 13 12 11 10
10 9 8 7 6 5 4 3 2 1

British Library Cataloguing in Publication Data
Bingham, Jane
Architecture. – (Culture in action)
720
A full catalogue record for this book is available from the British Library.

Acknowledgements
We would like to thank the following for permission to reproduce photographs: Alamy pp. 8 (© Ashley Cooper), **13 bottom** (©Picture Contact), **27** (©PCL); Corbis pp. **4** (Robert Harding World Imagery/ Neil Emmerson), **6** (Andrea Rugg Photography), **10** (Redlink/ Lo Mak), **11** (Richard Schulman), **18** (Bob Krist), **20** (Alan Schein Photography), **22** (Jim Zuckerman), **23** (Jose Fuste Raga), **24** (Richard A. Cooke), **26** (Arcaid/ Larraine Worpole); istockphoto pp. **5 top** (northlightimages ©Iain Sarjeant), **9** (©Steven Allan), **12** (© Branko Miokovic), **13 top** (© Marcus Clackson), **14** (© Todd Harrison), **16 top** (© Karim Hesham), **16 bottom** (© William D Fergus McNeill), **17** (© Jeremy Voisey), **19** (© einbo); Robert Harding p. **5 bottom** (Gavin Hellier); shutterstock p. **7** (©Jarne Gonzalez Zarraonandia).

Icon and banner images supplied by Shutterstock: © Alexander Lukin, © ornitopter, © Colorlife, and © David S. Rose.

Cover photograph of the Guggenheim Museum, Bilbao, reproduced with permission of Photolibrary (Rob Henderson).

We would like to thank Ryan Quinn Hines, Jackie Murphy, and Nancy Harris for their invaluable help in the preparation of this book.

Every effort has been made to contact copyright holders of material reproduced in this book. Any omissions will be rectified in subsequent printings if notice is given to the publishers.

Contents

Some words are printed in bold, **like this**. You can find out what they mean by looking in the glossary on page 30.

What is architecture?

When you hear the word architecture, what do you think of? Do you imagine a famous building, like the Sydney Opera House in Australia or the Eiffel Tower in Paris? Or do you picture a building you know well, such as your house or your school?

It doesn't matter what building you think of. Whenever you picture a building, you are thinking about architecture.

Architecture comes in many different forms. Which of these buildings is your favourite?

Architecture is everywhere

Architecture is just another word for buildings. Every time you walk along a street, you see architecture. Even a simple structure, like a bus shelter, has been designed by an **architect**.

Architects make regular visits to building sites to check that the builders are following their plan.

Architects at work

Architects sometimes say that they "make spaces". They design all kinds of structures, from houses and schools, to football stadiums and airports. An architect's job can be very exciting. Just imagine how you would feel if your drawing was turned into a real building!

Building a dream

The architect of the famous Sydney Opera House was inspired by the sailing boats in Sydney harbour. He decided to design a building made from the shapes of sails. It was a wonderful idea. But then he had to face the difficult challenge of turning his idea into reality!

The Sydney Opera House was designed in the 1950s by the Danish architect, Jørn Utzon.

What do architects do?

Architects have a challenging job. They must produce great-looking designs that are comfortable to live and work in, and their buildings must be safe and strong. Their design must please the **client** (the person who is paying them). They must also create a building that their client can afford!

Making good spaces

Architects need to think very carefully about the way their buildings will be used. Before an architect designs a school, he or she watches pupils and teachers in a school. This helps the architect to design the best possible spaces for work and play.

This is Wayzara School in Minnesota, United States. Would you like to go to school here?

Blending in or standing out?

Buildings do not exist on their own. Architects need to decide how their design works in its **environment**. Should the building blend into its surroundings? Or should it stand out and make a bold statement?

When architects make buildings to blend in with their surroundings, they need to think about many things. Will their design be too tall? Will its **style** (how it looks) stand out too much? And will its building **materials** blend in well?

Bold museum

Some modern buildings make very bold statements. But they can still look great in their environment. The Guggenheim Museum in Bilbao, Spain, looks like a giant, silver-coloured ship. It was carefully designed to look good in its waterside setting.

The Guggenheim Museum in Bilbao was designed by the American architect Frank O. Gehry. It was completed in 1997. Its thin strips of titanium are meant to look like fish scales.

Choosing a style

Architects have many building **styles** to choose from. Sometimes they copy a style that has been used in the past. For example, they might design a building in a **classical** (like the Parthenon in Athens) or a **Gothic** style (like Salisbury **Cathedral**). Sometimes they decide on a style that is new and unusual.

Which materials?

One of the choices that architects face is which **materials** to use. Should their building be made of brick, stone, wood, or steel? Or should they use some other material? The choice of materials depends on the style of the building and the way it will be used. Architects also need to think carefully about how their materials will fit into the **environment**.

In the forests of Scandinavia, people build timber houses with tiled roofs. The very steep roofs stop heavy snow from settling.

Traditional materials

Some materials have been used in buildings for thousands of years. Early forest dwellers made their homes from branches. People in hot, dry lands moulded buildings from mud. In bare, rocky places, people built shelters from stones. These traditional materials are all still used to construct buildings today.

Adobe buildings

People in desert regions often build their homes from adobe bricks. These are hand-made bricks made from a mixture of mud and straw. You can see adobe buildings in hot places like the American south-west and North Africa. Adobe buildings last for many years. They are often colourfully painted.

This adobe house is in New Mexico, United States. The house's thick mud walls keep it very cool inside.

The city of Shanghai, in China, is famous for its skyscrapers. Architects in Shanghai have used steel, concrete, and glass to create some amazing shapes.

Using concrete

Today, many architects use concrete in their buildings. Concrete is made from powdered rock, which is mixed with small stones and water. It is light but very strong.

Concrete can be poured into moulds (containers) of any shape. It can also be **reinforced** with iron rods. Reinforced concrete is used in skyscrapers because they need to be as light as possible.

Ancient concrete

Most people think that concrete is a modern invention. But it was invented almost 2,000 years ago! Roman builders mixed ashy soil from the slopes of volcanoes with wet lime. They used their new material to construct enormous buildings, like the Colosseum in Rome (see page 17).

Steel frames

Skyscrapers are built from concrete, steel, and glass. They have a frame of lightweight steel that bends very slightly in the wind. Skyscrapers have hundreds of windows, made from **toughened glass**. Some architects use coloured mirror-glass.

Using glass

Glass gives you views of the outside world and lets light into a building. It can be used in some very exciting ways. Some buildings are made entirely from glass. They are held together by frames of metal, wood, or plastic. Glass houses can range in size from simple garden houses to giant **pavilions** (large halls).

The architect Philip Johnson designed his Glass House in 1949. It is in the woods in New Canaan, Connecticut, United States. Why do you think he chose glass for this **environment**?

Making plans

Once an **architect** has decided on a design, it is time to draw up some plans. In the early stages of a project, architects make a few quick sketches to show their **client**. Later, they create detailed plans.

Different views

Architects show their designs in several different ways. They draw views of the building from each side. These side views are called **elevations**. They also show the floor plan of their building.

By looking at a floor plan, people can see the layout of the rooms. For a two-storey house, the architect would draw two floor plans – one for the downstairs and one for the upstairs.

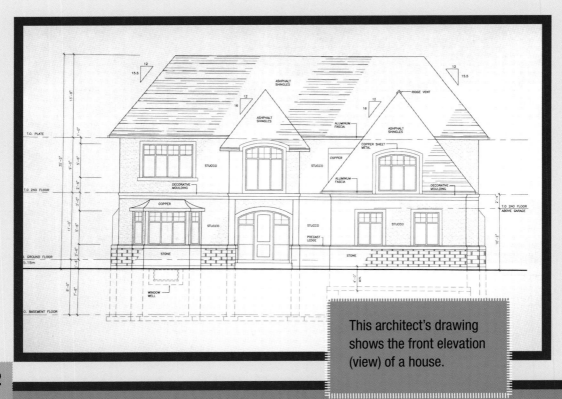

This architect's drawing shows the front elevation (view) of a house.

Making models

Some architects build models to show how their building will look. Today, many architects use computers to create **3-D** images of their design.

A model can help people to imagine a completed building.

Virtual buildings

It is possible to explore a building that has not yet been built! Architects can use computers to create a **virtual** building, that does not really exist. This allows people to take a tour through its rooms.

This architect is working on a virtual image of his building.

Drawing a floor plan

Architects draw floor plans to show how all the rooms in a building fit together. Each floor in a building is shown from above. Architects use special symbols to represent windows and doors.

This is an architect's floor plan. The architect has given measurements for each room.

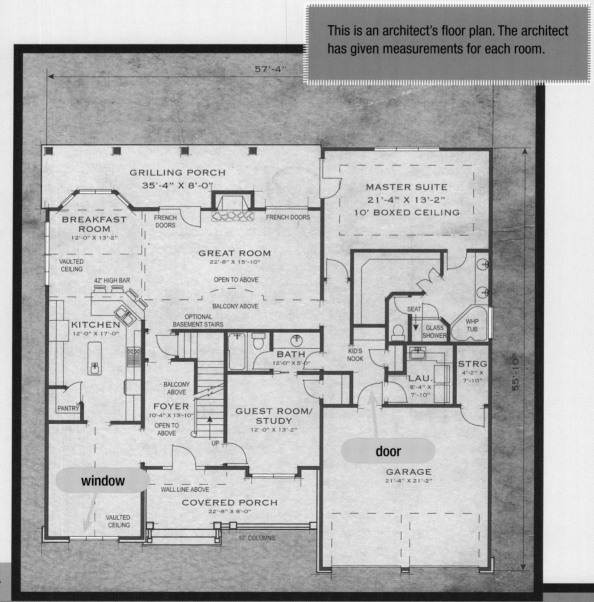

57'-4"

55'-10"

GRILLING PORCH
35'-4" X 8'-0"

MASTER SUITE
21'-4" X 13'-2"
10' BOXED CEILING

BREAKFAST ROOM
12'-0" X 13'-2"

FRENCH DOORS

FRENCH DOORS

VAULTED CEILING

GREAT ROOM
22'-8" X 15'-10"

OPEN TO ABOVE

42" HIGH BAR

SEAT

BALCONY ABOVE

GLASS SHOWER

WHP TUB

KITCHEN
12'-0" X 17'-0"

OPTIONAL BASEMENT STAIRS

BATH
12'-0" X 5'-0"

KID'S NOOK

LAU.
8'-4" X 7'-10"

STRG
4'-2" X 7'-10"

BALCONY ABOVE

PANTRY

FOYER
10'-4" X 13'-10"

OPEN TO ABOVE

UP

GUEST ROOM/ STUDY
12'-0" X 13'-2"

door

GARAGE
21'-4" X 21'-2"

window

WALL LINE ABOVE

COVERED PORCH
22'-8" X 8'-0"

VAULTED CEILING

10" COLUMNS

Design your dream house

What would your dream house look like? Would it look like a house you know? Or would it be very unusual?

Imagine that you are an architect showing the plans of your house to a **client**. The plans will help them picture exactly how your dream house will look.

Steps to follow:

1. First draw your dream house from the front. This is called a front **elevation**.

2. Look at the floor plan on page 14. Do you want a breakfast room or study in your dream house? Then create a floor plan of your own to show the rooms on the ground floor.

This is the front elevation. You may also want to show a back and side elevation.

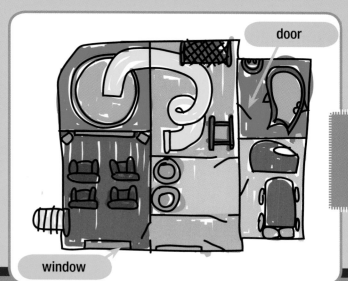

door

window

This is the floor plan of the ground floor. If your house has more than one floor, draw floor plans for them, too.

Brilliant buildings

People have been designing buildings for thousands of years. In this chapter, you can see examples of a few great buildings. Some of the designs are so good that they are still copied today.

Egyptian pyramids

The ancient Egyptians built huge stone **tombs** in the shape of pyramids. They began with a square base. Then they added more and more levels, each one smaller than the one below. When the pyramid was complete, they covered each side with a thin sheet of polished stone.

The Great Pyramid in Giza, Egypt, was built 4,600 years ago.

Greek temples

The ancient Greeks built large, rectangular buildings. These buildings were **temples** where priests held religious **ceremonies**. The Greeks used rows of **columns** to support the temple roof. Greek temples were decorated with carvings showing gods and goddesses.

The Parthenon in Athens was one of the Greeks' most important temples.

Roman amphitheatres

The Romans copied the Greeks' building **style**. They also introduced some new features of their own. One important feature was the rounded **arch**. Walls with arches are strong and light. You can build several layers of arches on top of each other. The word "architecture" comes from "arch".

The Romans used arches in most of their buildings. One of their most spectacular structures was the **amphitheatre**. Roman amphitheatres were huge stadiums, used for sports and entertainment.

arch

The Colosseum in Rome was the largest of the Roman amphitheatres. It could hold up to 50,000 people.

Classical columns

The Greek and Roman building style is known as **classical** architecture. Classical buildings have three main types of column: Doric, Ionic, and Corinthian.

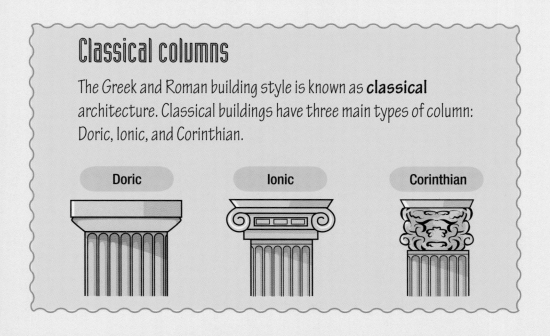

Doric　　　　　Ionic　　　　　Corinthian

Pagodas from Asia

During the first century CE, people in China began to build tall **temples**. The temples were made from wood and had many roofs. These temple towers are known as **pagodas**. There are pagodas in many countries of the Far East, including China, Japan, Korea, and Thailand. Pagodas can survive earthquakes, because their wooden structure sways but does not break.

Longhua pagoda in China dates from the 900s CE. Like many Chinese pagodas, it is **octagonal** (has eight sides).

minaret

The Taj Mahal in India is one of the most famous examples of Islamic architecture. It is made from white marble. It was built between 1632 and 1653 as a tomb for Emperor Shah Jahan's wife.

Islamic architecture

The religion of Islam began in the Middle East in the 600s CE. **Muslims** built **mosques** where people could worship and **tombs** where people were buried. These buildings had rounded roofs, called **domes**, and tall towers called **minarets**. Many Islamic buildings are decorated with carvings and coloured tiles.

Christian cathedrals

In the 1000s CE, people in Europe began to build **cathedrals**. These are very large buildings where **Christians** meet to worship. Cathedrals are decorated with carvings. They have tall windows filled with colourful **stained glass**.

Romanesque and Gothic

The early cathedrals were built in a **Romanesque** style. They had rounded **arches** copied from the Romans. By 1200 CE, the lighter **Gothic** style was popular. Gothic cathedrals have pointed arches and **spires** (tall, pointed roofs).

Skyscrapers

The first skyscraper was built in Chicago, United States, in 1885. It was 10 floors high, but people were soon building much taller buildings. In 1931, the Empire State Building was built in New York. It was the first skyscraper to have more than 100 floors.

The Empire State Building measures 381 metres (1,250 feet). Today, the world's tallest skyscraper is the Taipei 101 building in Taiwan. It is 509 metres (1,671 feet) tall. More than 10,000 people work in it every day. The Burg Tower in Dubai could soon overtake Taipei 101 as the world's tallest skyscraper.

For 40 years, the Empire State Building was the world's tallest skyscraper.

Making shapes

All the buildings pictured in this chapter have very interesting shapes. In this mime activity, you use your body to create building shapes.

Steps to follow:

1. First practise miming some different building shapes. Some shapes are quite easy to make on your own. For other buildings it is best to work in pairs or groups. (Be careful when you are miming tall buildings!)

2. Divide into two teams, and take turns guessing what the other team is miming.

3. When you have mimed all the buildings in this chapter, you could try making the shapes of other buildings you know.

Great architects

Nobody knows who designed the Great Pyramid, but we do know the names of some great **architects**. This chapter looks at the work of a few outstanding architects, from the 1400s to the present day.

Filippo Brunelleschi

Filippo Brunelleschi lived in Italy in the 1400s. He studied ancient Roman buildings and taught himself to design in the **classical style**. Brunelleschi designed many classical buildings. His most famous work was a **dome** for Florence's **cathedral**.

Brunelleschi's dome for Florence Cathedral was completed in 1436. It was the first **octagonal** dome in history.

Sir Christopher Wren

Sir Christopher Wren was an English architect. He designed buildings in the classical style. In 1666 the Great Fire of London destroyed the old St. Paul's Cathedral. Wren designed the new cathedral, as well as over 50 London churches.

Antoni Gaudí

Antoni Gaudí lived and worked in Spain around the beginning of the 1900s. He was inspired by the shapes of plants. Gaudi's buildings look rather like sculptures. Their surfaces are covered with carvings and mosaics. Mosaics are made up of many small pieces of coloured stone or glass.

Gaudí's most famous building is the cathedral of *La Sagrada Familia* in the city of Barcelona, Spain. He started his cathedral in 1882, and worked on it for 44 years, right up until his death. The cathedral is still unfinished today.

Gaudí designed 18 **spires** for *La Sagrada Familia*.

One of Frank Lloyd Wright's most famous designs is Fallingwater, in Pennsylvania, United States. The house was built above a waterfall.

Frank Lloyd Wright

Frank Lloyd Wright worked in America in the early 1900s. He was inspired by nature, and he tried to make his buildings fit in naturally with their surroundings.

Zaha Hadid

Zaha Hadid was born in Iraq in 1950. Now she lives in London, but she has designed buildings all around the world. Most of her designs have very unusual shapes, such as the BMW Central Building in Germany..

Music for buildings

When the **dome** of Florence **Cathedral** was finished, the **composer** Dufay wrote a special piece of music. Dufay's music was in honour of Brunelleschi's masterpiece. He tried to make his music express the spirit of the new dome.

In this activity, you can express the spirit of different buildings, using rhythm, music, voice, and dance.

Steps to follow:

1. Start by creating music and dance to express the spirit of Frank Lloyd Wright's Fallingwater. You can beat a rhythm with your hands and use your voice to make the sounds of water. Or you can use instruments like recorders and drums.

2. Now choose a different kind of building. You could create music and dance for:
   - Florence Cathedral (see page 22)
   - *La Sagrada Familia* (see page 23)

3. Think of a building you know well and create music and dance for it.

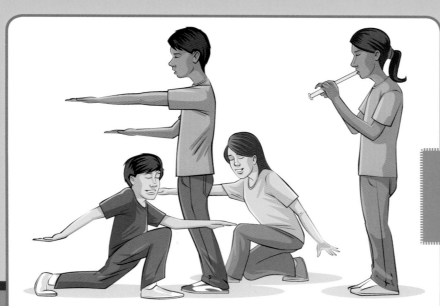

This group is imitating the spirit of Fallingwater and its waterfalls.

What next?

Architecture is changing very quickly. Today's **architects** are using new **materials** and building skills to create some very exciting new structures.

Green buildings

Many architects today are trying to create "green buildings". These green designs are intended to use as little **energy** as possible. Green buildings are sometimes known as **eco-homes**. They have many energy-saving features, such as **solar panels**. Solar panels use energy from the sun to heat the house.

Some eco-buildings are built partly underground. This means that they stay much warmer in winter, and cooler in summer. Many architects of green buildings use natural materials and create designs that blend into the **environment**.

In the future, "green" designs will probably become much more common. This eco-home is built into the side of a hill.

All change

What will the buildings of the future look like? It is impossible to know, but one thing is certain. Architects will keep trying out new materials, **styles**, and ideas.

Inside-out

Some modern architects have created a new kind of building. These buildings have all their water pipes, lifts, and stairs on the outside. This leaves very large spaces inside. These unusual buildings are sometimes known as "inside-out" designs.

The Lloyds Building in London was designed by Sir Richard Rogers. All its pipes and lifts are on the outside.

Sir Richard Rogers (b. 1933)

Sir Richard Rogers is a British architect who is famous for his "inside-out" designs. His buildings include the Pompidou Centre in Paris, the Lloyd's Building, and the Millennium **Dome** in London.

Timeline

BCE	
Around 3,500	The wheel is invented in the Middle East.
Around 2,600	The Great Pyramid is built in ancient Egypt.
Around 800	The ancient Greek **civilization** begins.
Around 750	The city of Rome is founded.
Around 432	The Parthenon is completed in Athens, Greece.
27	The Roman Empire begins.

CE	
68	The first **pagoda** is built in China.
80	The Colosseum is completed in Rome.
476	The Roman Empire collapses.
977	Longhua pagoda is built in China.
1320	Salisbury **Cathedral** is completed in England.
1436	The **dome** of Florence Cathedral is completed in Italy.
1492	Christopher Columbus reaches America.
1653	The Taj Mahal is completed in India.
1789	The French Revolution begins.
1865	The American Civil War ends.

1882	Antoni Gaudí starts work on *La Sagrada Familia* cathedral.
1885	The first skyscraper is built in the United States.
1914–1918	World War I.
1931	The Empire State Building is completed in New York, USA.
1935	Frank Lloyd Wright designs Fallingwater in America.
1939–1945	World War II.
1957	Jørn Utzon wins a competition to design the Sydney Opera House in Australia.
1969	The first man walks on the moon.
1986	Sir Richard Rogers' Lloyds Building is completed in London.
1997	Frank O. Gehry's Guggenheim Museum is completed in Spain.
2001	Terrorists fly planes into the Twin Towers of the World Trade Center in New York, USA.
2004	The Taipei 101 skyscraper is completed in Taiwan. It becomes the world's tallest building.
	Zaha Hadid becomes the first woman to win the Pritzker Prize for architecture.
2006	Zaha Hadid designs Dancing Towers to be built in Dubai.
2009	The Burg Dubai is predicted to become the world's tallest skyscraper.

Glossary

3-D three dimensional. A 3-D shape has three dimensions (length, width, and depth).

amphitheatre large, open-air stadium where people in Roman times went for entertainment

arch curved structure, often used to help support a building or bridge

architect person who designs buildings, and makes sure they are being constructed correctly

cathedral large and important church, where Christians worship

ceremony actions, words, and music performed to mark a special occasion

Christian someone who worships Jesus Christ, and believes he is the son of God

civilization society with a high level of art, science, and government

classical style of ancient Greece or Rome

client someone who pays an expert, such as an architect, to do a job for them

column tall, upright pillar supporting a building

composer someone who writes music

dome rounded roof

eco-home buildings that have energy saving features, such as solar panels

elevation view of a building from one side

energy resource that makes something work

environment things that make a place special and different. A modern glass building might look good in a city, but not in the countryside.

Gothic in the style used in western Europe between around 1000 and 1450 CE. Gothic buildings have tall, pointed arches.

material thing used to make a building. Materials for buildings could be mud, stone, wood, steel, or other man-made substances.

minaret slender tower. A minaret has a balcony from which Muslims are called to prayer.

mosque building where Muslims worship

Muslim someone who follows the religion of Islam

octagonal having eight sides

pagoda tower with many roofs, built to be used as temples. Pagodas are found in many parts of Asia.

pavilion very large hall where exhibitions are held

reinforced strengthened

Romanesque in the style used in western Europe between around 800 and 1000 CE. Romanesque buildings have rounded arches.

solar panel panel that collects energy from the Sun, and uses it for heating and lighting. Solar panels are often placed on the roofs of buildings.

spire very tall, pointed roofs

stained glass coloured glass used in windows, usually in churches and cathedrals

style how something looks. Buildings can have many different styles.

temple building used for worship

tomb grave, usually for an important person

toughened glass glass that is treated in a factory to make it extremely strong

virtual something that seems real, but does not actually exist

Find out more

Books

How to Draw Buildings (*Young Artist*), Pam Beasant (Usborne Books, 2006)
Learn how to draw your own buildings, using examples from all over the world.

Skyscrapers (*Building Amazing Structures*), Chris Oxlade (Heinemann Library, 2006)
This book explores the development of skyscrapers throughout history, shows how they are built, and asks what they are used for.

The Picture History of Great Buildings, Gillian Clements (Frances Lincoln, 2007)
Each page of this book looks at one building and examines its history, its builders, and the impact its **style** had on later buildings.

Websites

Architecture for Kids
www.takus.com/architecture
This website about architectural history concentrates on American houses.

Archkidecture
www.archkidecture.org
A great introduction to architecture for children. The site includes suggestions for practical projects.

The Great Buildings Collection
www.greatbuildings.com/gbc/buildings
This site has pictures and information on over 750 buildings and their **architects**. You can search the database by place, date, building type, or architect name.

Places to visit

St Paul's Cathedral
St Paul's Churchyard
London EC4M 8AD
Tel: +44 (0)20 7246 8350 or +44(0)20 7236 4128
www.stpauls.co.uk
St Paul's Cathedral has towered over London since 604 CE, in various forms!

The Eiffel Tower
Tour Eiffel
Champ de Mars
75007 Paris
Tel: 33 (0) 1 44 54 19 30
www.tour-eiffel.fr/teiffel/uk
Follow Gus's yellow trainer soles for a tour of the first floor of the Eiffel Tower!

Index

PILLGWENLLY

26-07-18